Foreword
Ezekiel Leke Ojo, FCA
Senior Pastor, RCCG Solid Rock Phoenix, Arizona

BREAKING
THE CYCLE OF
INSUFFICIENCY

Godfrey O. Ekhomu, CPA
Author of Financial Maturity after the Recession

We want to hear from you. Please send your comments about this book to us in care of the address at the last page. Thank you.

Breaking the Cycle of Insufficiency

Paperback ISBN 978-0-9910359-0-8
eBook ISBN 978-0-9910359-1-5

Published by
Godkulture Publishing
Chicago, Illinois

Phone: 773-696-0008
Email: publishing@godkulture.org
www.godkulturepublishing.com

Printed in the United States of America

This book is dedicated to those believers who believe that Christ causes them to win always in all areas of life including poverty, struggle, uncertainty, broke, fear, lack, toil....

Acknowledgements

I am forever grateful to God for being the head of my life and for directing me in all my undertakings. I cannot resist His guidance and instructions at all times. Much thanks to my Pastor Leke Adesanya, your first visit to the U.S. was a blast! To my Chicago Pastor Dr. Kay Ijisesan, always challenging me to aspire and achieve more, while teaching me the elements of Supernatural lifestyle. Also I extend gratitude to all my callers on the "Looking Up to Jesus" phone ministry.

To an awesome laborer for Jesus Christ, Pastor Leke Ojo, who graciously wrote the Foreword to the book. I am equally grateful to my siblings and friends, and cousins in Chicago and all over the USA. Thanks to the United Esan Association for their support. And specifically to those who worked directly with me on this book - Gina Hernandez and Bridget Omogiate; definitely, last but not the least, Aquilla Omofoma Ekhomu, my biggest fan.

I am Grateful!

Contents

Foreword

John 10:10 says: *The thief cometh not, but for to steal, and to kill, and to destroy: I am come that they might have life and that they might have it more abundantly.*

Insufficiency can be simply defined as "a state of shortage of supply below what is required." There is a spirit behind insufficiency and that spirit is a direct negation of the above scripture. God is not the author of lack but the God of all sufficiency.

In this book, Pastor Godfrey did an excellent job, exposing the secrets of the spirit of insufficiency. When he wrote about the financial siege, he aptly captured the whole essence of our liberty from the twin bondage of lack and insufficiency. If readers can pay close attention to the factors responsible for insufficiency and apply the antidotes he proffered; then the life of abundance will not be a mirage to many.

The climax of the book was when he metaphorically identified the various avenues, ways, streets, lanes and boulevards that characterized the "city of insufficiency."

If people can deliberately avoid them; then life will begin to have meanings. For those that are thinking of going into business but are scared of lack of capital; the two chapters on budget and raising capital will be very helpful.

As we embark on the journey towards total liberty, this book is an excellent resource for the body of Christ and those that are under the suffocating oppression of the spirit of insufficiency.

Happy reading!

Ezekiel Leke Ojo, FCA
Senior Pastor
RCCG Solid Rock Phoenix
Arizona

Preface

A generation has not been born without some type of challenge. Each generation faces one challenge or another, and yet the generation survives in the end. In each case that generation dealt with a particular situation. Well, welcome to this new generation where the children of Light are engaged in exploits and producing Kingdom-minded solutions.

This book, *Breaking the Cycle of Insufficiency*, addresses obstacles positioned to intimidate and embarrass the children of God. A great percentage of Christians are vibrantly opposed to the doctrine of insufficiency and lack, and yet the enemy attacks this area of their finances to bring them to their knees and create destabilization in various areas of their life.

I have presented three solutions to assist you, the reader, to walk in victory. These solutions are very practical and attainable and there are real life testimonies to buttress the viability of each solution discussed here. The solution relating to intangibility stresses the comfort of having God on your side. The second solution gives 21 ways to raise capital (cash) for your ventures (personal or business). Each way describes a practical approach for implementation. The third solution deals with the ability to conform to budgeting standards and practicing budgeting with great delight.

This book is a solution for our generation, especially for believers struggling financially. Each chapter gives a picture, depicting its essence with bullet points, to provide ease to the reader. Today, I declare the end to your financial struggles in the Name of Jesus, Amen!

Pastor Godfrey O. Ekhomu, CPA
July 1, 2013

Chapter *1*
Miry Clay
(Financial Siege)

Highlights

- Financial Siege
- Business Insufficiency

FINANCIAL SIEGE

ALMOST AND ALWAYS, we find ourselves in a financial 'miry clay.' Financial miry clay deals specifically with our financial condition. The person in financial miry clay experiences a devastating financial disorder, whereby the individual goes through a financial mess. This financial mess could be very devastating and could create a cycle that could almost be very vicious. The results are bankruptcy, foreclosure or eviction, unemployment, and a mountain of bills. Then there are the phone calls! Phone calls from the bill collection agencies are less than friendly and mostly insulting. Some people go as far as asking their children to answer such calls and lie about their whereabouts. These types of lies would grant the enemy additional foothold into their financial miry clay.

Lately, the embarrassing collection calls have become the norm at the work place. Collection agents are now calling people in financial disorder on their jobs; the frequency of such calls is much, and they trigger supervisor intervention that might lead to embarrassment or termination. During my work tenure at a company in 2012, two employees were terminated because they were constantly on the phone. When I enquired into the nature of their termination from the other employees, they informed me that the company raised queries regarding their excessive telephone usage for personal financial matters with collection agents.

This is a condition no one would wish on anyone.

> *He brought me up also out of an horrible pit, out of the miry clay, and set my feet upon a rock, [and] established my goings* (Psalms 40:1).

King David describes in vivid terms the dire conditions in miry clay. He noted that it was a "horrible pit." The use of the term horrible shows the condition that David was in. The condition was painful and sad, which was equivalent to being in a state of hopelessness. In other words, it could be said that the conditions were depressing, oppressing, suppressing, repressing, compressing, and down-casting. While David was not necessarily speaking of the financial conditions in his home, he probably was addressing the challenges in his family. In today's interpretation, it is needful to see that this horrible pit can refer to a state of financial horror. And any financial horror affects the effectiveness of a family. A family lacking a good financial agenda or plan-runs a risk of being broken up because the enemy would have found a foothold, as described earlier. The good news is that the Lord set David's feet upon a rock. This is definitely something to shout about! There is a need for people to understand the essence of positive confession in the process of faith formation for freedom.

In the business world, the financial representative *calls* the Statement of Financial Position the Balance

Sheet; meaning that there needs to be a balance in the financial representation of the organization, where assets would equal liabilities and equity. Similarly, there is a need to have balance in the financial habits of a family. A company that has a negative equity position is functionally bankrupt. No one wants to do business with that company. That's the awareness that individuals should have. When the individual's balance sheet is upside down, no entity is interested in doing business with the individual and that creates financial discomfort for everyone involved.

The financial state of many people, presently, is very disturbing. Their financial state is justifiably tight because their financial inflow does not match the outflow. The technical word for this is "deficit." Each time you want to purchase an item for your home, you cringe because you are concerned that the purchase might be declined. A few months back a Christian brother called and complained bitterly about this his financial condition. I could relate with what he was saying because I had experienced a similar situation 10 years earlier. His condition was dire and that forced him to file for bankruptcy. Well, I didn't like that and I expressed my displeasure and I still stand by that. He was experiencing a major financial siege in his life.

In the natural, the likelihood of him overcoming the situation was nil. I was unable to ascribe blame to him because natural conditions are more real to most of us than the supernatural. The natural is what we see, hear and experience daily. Therefore, because of our intimate knowledge of the natural, it is hard for us to believe anything under the realm of the supernatural and anyone who ministers the supernatural to us is merely wasting our time and speaking words that do not have hope for manifestation. My friend knew the Lord, but his financial siege made him doubt God's ability to help him triumph. The truth of the matter is that this brother was experiencing a financial siege.

> *David therefore departed thence, and escaped to the cave Adullam: and when his brethren and all his father's house heard [it], they went down thither to him* (1 Samuel 22:1).

David found himself in a cave, under siege when he was doing all he could to escape the wrath of King Saul. The cave became a stronghold where he had to hide. It was during his besiegement that he consolidated his military strength and started to advance his might. Beecher (2004) writes "In our current speech "cave of Adullam" suggests an aggregation of ill-assorted and disreputable men. This is not justified by the Bible record. David's men included his numerous and respectable kinsmen, and the representative of the priesthood, and some of David's military companions, and some men who afterward held high office in Israel. Even those who are described as being in distress and debt and bitter of soul were doubtless, many of them, persons who had suffered at the hands of Saul on account of their friendship for David. Doubtless they included mere adventurers in their number; but the Scriptural details and the circumstances alike indicate that they were mainly homogeneous and that most of them were worthy citizens."

Like David and his men, we too, can face a siege; financial siege is almost a battle we all must fight in life. Those who undergo financial siege are good and decent people, mostly. They are being attacked by the enemy. They are worthy citizens who are besieged by the errors of life. In many instances, the circumstances that landed them in a financial mess are bigger than them. They fought hard to stay out of the problems. Their valiant efforts didn't bring them victory. Although their efforts looked lame, they tried. That's not to say others have not been deliberate squanderers. These deliberate perpetrators failed to see the avalanche of financial problems. They miscalculated and misused their blessings. Even at the point of grace, God granted them a reprieve but they returned back to the place of crime. They dabbled in what they should not have dabbled in. And so they fell back to where they started. God sees them and still grants them grace in time of need.

These are God's special children. Even when they know that they are blatantly wrong in their financial decisions, they still trust in the Lord their God to do exploits. In view of this, Daniel wrote, "...*but the people that do know their God shall be strong, and do exploits* (Daniel 11:32). In

17

their financial mess, these special ones still find ways to stay afloat. They may be stretched, but are not breakable. Yes, they get calls from the creditors and receive lots of letters from them, but they never give up. They find ways to make things happen in life. That's what they have signed up for. They want to get out but somehow they are trapped, and God knows because God has a solution for them.

BUSINESS INSUFFICIENCY

Too many times when we talk of breaking the cycle of insufficiency we focus on individuals only. It needs a balance. There are business insufficiencies, especially for those individuals who are run their own businesses. Also, for those who have less than adequate capitalization, due to the fact that a business is not adequately funded, could create a huge setback for the success of the business. Many businesses fail to retain their earnings and they are unable to do things that would enlarge the business.

Sadly, most of them will operate on a deficit basis and actually consider filing for bankruptcy. A business that will thrive must be conscientious about its spending habits and must work in concert with a financial specialist to curtail costs and to ensure that all monies to be spent have a budget assignment. A business that fails to budget is a business that invites failure. There are situations where a business has a budget, but there is constant budget override. When those who have overriding abilities override the business budget, bad things normally happen.

In the case of a really small business, when the expenses outweigh the income or revenue, the accountant must raise a red flag and bring this topic to the attention of the 'powers that be' or business owners. The accountant should take all steps to ensure that the existing problem is solved. Companies are established to make money. They must keep their focus to make money and ensure the products or services are yielding income. The first law of defeating corporate insufficiency is to curtail excessive spending. When the organization brings spending under control, everything else would fall in place. Corporate insufficiency does not need to exist. A corporate surplus is a must and must be encouraged. When an organization does not have sufficient capital, the organization will not be able to fund basic organizational needs such as property, plant and equipment, and more importantly inventory for resale. Since organizations cannot seek financial relief through personal channels, I have included several loan options to help organizations in Chapter 7 of this book. The organization should pay attention to loans that would be able to help them. However, it is more advisable that the organization should use its reserves instead of borrowing.

Chapter 2
Reasons For
Financial Siege

Highlights

- Inadequate Income
- Excessive Income Outflow
- Failure to Prioritize
- Abandoning Prophetic Instructions
- Giving Into Ungodly Habit
- Failure to Hate what God hates

In researching this area of the book, I discovered some reasons why we encounter a financial siege or are trapped in financial miry clay.

INADEQUATE INCOME

This happens when we don't bring in enough income. This is common to everyone and with everyone undergoing the insufficiency syndrome. Most people we know do not make a lot of money. In a household of four family members, it has become a trend that only one has a job. The work itself does not pay much, and so the family struggles through daily living and spending. There are cases where they may qualify for government assistance, however, due to the fact that the government is broke as well, they receive very low government help, or at times, do not receive anything at all. When the family has no one working, the pain is higher and problems created are very real and the evidence of a "horrible pit" is not disputable.

An Inadequate financial pool occurs when we do not have enough money to satisfy our obligations. This season is driven by lack of adequate inflow to support the daily spending ambition of an individual. This is often the result of a lack of employment or when sufficient money is not being made from being self-employed. People rely mainly on employers or their jobs to satisfy their financial needs. Most workers work an average of 40 hours per week. Due to recent national economic struggles, it has become harder to even get 40 hours work week. Prayerfully, the hourly rate can help cover your bills.

Here is an analogy. Anthony worked as an associate with BP Oil. He made $20 per hour. In 40 hours he made $800 for the week. His net income after taxes (20%) was $640. In one month, Anthony's income was $2,560. Benson operated a small business on 75th and Main Street in Phoenix. At the end of every week, his tape register recorded $650 in Revenue. Assuming Benson paid out 5% in State sales tax, his net would be $2,470 for the month. For the two examples above, the monthly incomes appear low because Brother Anthony's annual income is $30,720 and Benson's is $29,640. If they have expenses greater than $30,000, they both would find themselves in financial hardship.

EXCESSIVE INCOME OUTFLOW

This arises when we spend more than we bring in. This creates more problems for family members than anything else. Those facing financial disorder might end up over-spending. When they over-spend, they immediately trigger the law of deficit. Deficit occurs when your spending exceeds your income. All the indicators show that bad things are about to happen. In the family, the adults would feud about who did the most spending. When adults fight, there is instability in the family. This could lead to more devastating consequences.

Spending too much by using the example discussed above suggests that when Benson or Anthony incurs more expenses than their set income, hardship becomes inevitable. People need to bring their spending under control in order to avoid financial stress. A financial stress can create discomfort in many ways. God has not called us unto discomfort. We need to learn to streamline and stay within our buying power. Many people have abused the intent of the Bible. They have quoted and misquoted James the half-brother of Jesus Christ in many different ways.

> ... *count it all joy when ye fall into divers temptations* (James 1:2).

The divers temptations we fall into do not include self-instigated problems. When you over-spend or issue bad checks, more than likely, you could receive a visit from the FBI for check schemes. James was not endorsing these conducts. Please do not say "count it all joy" because James was talking of "divers temptations" instigated by God. There are situations that have been designed to test our faith and patience; they are designed to help us to be responsible. The good news is that God makes a way of escape when we fall into such diverse trials.

FAILURE TO PRIORITIZE

The overall law regarding the prioritization of inflow and outflow is planning and control, which is budgeting.

Budgeting is a management tool that measures performance. As a management tool, a budget manager uses the budget to examine inflow and outflow patterns of the family income and expenses. The budget manager also examines the performance of each budgetary angle to express a level of confidence or a need to adjust accordingly. Each budget manager is held accountable for the resulting outcome of the budget. The resulting outcome of the budget defines the next level for that manager. The manager is either promoted for a good budget handling, or punished for mishandling the budget. Some families fail to budget. This failure creates unneeded tension in the family especially when the family is operating in the red. A home that refuses to budget will struggle a lot because there are no measuring guidelines to enforce the discipline in spending.

ABANDONING PROPHETIC INSTRUCTIONS

People experience financial siege because they fail to act upon a prophetic word given to them. In some cases people fail to receive the prophetic declaration and do not follow through. They either ignore the declaration or call the declaration nonsensical. In May of 2013, by the leading of the Holy Spirit, I asked people on our telephone prayer line to pick 5 stones and keep for the month. The leading was that the number five represents grace. Also, it was revealed that David picked out 5 stones to fight and defeat Goliath of Gath. Some people carried out the instruction, and others failed to do so. There were several testimonies from those who followed the instructions. Of those who did not follow the instruction, one came back and said she was unsure of the basis of the instruction; as such she refused to follow. She also indicated that she has this special relationship with the Holy Ghost and she would only take instructions from Him thereof. Well you can guess how that ended. The Bible states in 2 Chronicles 20:20.

Jehoshaphat stood and said, Hear me, O Judah, and ye inhabitants of Jerusalem; Believe in the LORD your God, so shall ye be established; believe his prophets, so shall ye prosper.

This scripture supports the notion that God would send His prophet to declare certain words that are liberating to man. Those who receive and execute the instructions as given are beneficiaries of God's inheritance.

GIVING INTO UNGODLY HABITS

The fifth reason why people are trapped in financial miry clay is, accommodating ungodly habits. In my book, *Financial Maturity after the Recession*, I wrote the following regarding ungodly habit. "Bad habits are the worst. They can really lead you into debt. Many years ago, I was dealing with a bad habit and so I borrowed from my 401k, paycheck, even from individuals in order to support my habit. Bad habits are hard to beat. I speak from experience. And so I do not condemn you struggling from one addiction or another. My prayers are with you."

Given this, Paul the apostle wrote to the Galatians and us, saying that:

> *Stand fast therefore in the liberty wherewith Christ hath made us free, and be not entangled again with the yoke of bondage* (Galatians 5:1).

I admonish you to stand fast in your freedom. Your absolute freedom from addiction is certain. If you are struggling from ANY form of addiction, I highly suggest you commit this verse to memory. Post it on your refrigerator; post it in your bedroom and everywhere you can see and read it. It works. It really works...

The costs of bad habits could add up fast. You will find yourself in full denial and blame everyone and everything about your piling debt. If you used your paycheck to pay your bills, you will not have piling debts. A pastor once said to me "it is not how much money you make that matters, it is what you do with what you make." He was so right. I made so much money but did not use it wisely. If you are reading this book on the plane, in your house, traveling, or anywhere; just stop and ask yourself what habit can you drop today?

FAILURE TO HATE WHAT GOD HATES

A key challenge that arises for those entangled with financial woes is their failure to hate the things that God hates. It is needful that we hate the things that upset God.

For instance, Clarke's Commentary on Proverbs 6:16 states that:

These six doth the Lord hate – plus one
(a) A proud look - exalted eyes; those who will not condescend to look on the rest of mankind.
(b) A lying tongue - he who neither loves nor tells truth.
(c) Hands that shed innocent blood, whether by murder or by battery.
(d) A heart that deviseth wicked imaginations - the heart that fabricates such, lays the foundation, builds upon it, and completes the superstructure of iniquity.
(e) Feet that be swift in running to mischief - he who works iniquity with greediness.
(f) A false witness that speaketh lies - one who, even on his oath before a court of justice, tells anything but the truth.
(g) Seven are an abomination unto him - "to his soul." The seventh is, he that soweth discord among brethren - he who troubles the peace of a family, of a village, of the state; all who, by lies and misrepresentations, strive to make men's minds evil-affected towards their brethren.

Are you desisting from such? If not, you can begin right now so that you can have a good foundation.

Chapter 3
Streets to Avoid

Highlights

- Poverty Avenue
- The Struggle Way
- Uncertainty Street
- Broke Lane
- Fear Boulevard
- Paycheck Circle
- Lack Junction

In the era of wealth dispensation, it is important to note that basic confessions and locations as well as habitation become very important. Too many people have dwelt in the erroneous dispensation of religiosity. One can even argue that religiosity presents or positions itself as false humility. They accept certain names and proclaim they are full of humble attitudes. I disagree! The 'street' you live on determines your destiny and as such it is important that you watch where you live in order for your destiny not to be compromised. This book talks about attacking this particular cycle of insufficiency. In it, I highlight the desperate nature of people's inability to get liberated from their dire financial situation. There are seven streets we must avoid living in, they are:

POVERTY AVENUE

This has to be one of the most tormented avenues on earth. There is nothing good about being poor. Poverty is a disease that must be cured. A man who wakes up at 7am and goes after a bottle of beer and then drinks all day, with a distorted life is sick and is called an alcoholic. This is the same as someone who lives in a poor state. Poverty needs to be cured by an extensive attack on the root of Poverty Avenue. In light of this, Psalms 11:3 states that, *"If the foundations be destroyed, what can the righteous do?"* The foundation of a righteous person can be exposed to certain life inadequacies. Unless these life inadequacies are attacked, the person continuously goes in a never-ending cycle. A repeated pattern is not usually a sane pattern. Doing the same thing over and over again is said to be insanity. The last time the Bible repeated itself over and over again, there was a tremendous breakthrough for a testimony. Please refer to Ezekiel 21:27.

> *I will overturn, overturn, overturn, it: and it shall be no [more], until he come whose right it is; and I will give it [him].*

Pastor Courage Igene (2013) in his book, *100 Reasons Why I hate Poverty*, decried the elements of poverty; he indicated that poverty is not something to be proud of. He said poverty should be attacked with all vigor and strength. This street of poverty should be rendered null and void because we have overcome! An overcomer does not walk in disbelief; does not rest, and does not live in poverty. It is noted here, that poverty could be in another form other than money, but in whichever form it presents itself, it must be eradicated.

STRUGGLE WAY

Everyone on the path of Struggle Way needs particular and specific attention from God. Struggle Way deals with one's inability to make that turn. In struggle way mentality, there are lots of issues to deal with. Struggle Way has no testimony and is a dead end situation. People in Struggle Way end up blaming someone else for their situation! They blame it on race, nationality, language, income level, parents, significant other or spouses, on their children, on family, friends and foes. Never in their life do they ever blame anything on themselves. There is an attitude of entitlement that has failed; that attitude tends to crumble their desire for liberation. In Struggle Way, the residents are always unhappy and then they blame God for their residence in the street that they are in. When you minister the Word of God to them, they answer you with a question such as "Where was God when I was blah…blah…blah… "

Struggle Way folks need a special deliverance service targeted at them. The concern I harbor in my heart is that these individuals walk in absolute bitterness, strife and unforgiveness. Ask them, they will disagree with you but probe a little further and the truth will show up. As my reader, you may disagree but that is my position; nevertheless, I challenge you to disprove it in your own book! I trust this will serve as a challenge for you to write your own book. When I read Dr. Festus Adeyeye's book, *Prospering during Hard Times*, I was able to conclude that prayers are very essential for those in this street.

UNCERTAINTY STREET

Those that live in this street have all kinds of doubts built into their system. They never can determine or decide whether this financial venture belongs to them or not. They are always unsure whether to proceed or not. They live in a cycle of doubting their best resolution. In this street, confidence can wear thin quickly. It could be said that they were engaged in a project or a deal that failed and because of that scare, they are discouraged to trust the next opportunity. They would ask questions about specific projects and when the answer is given, they will cast it down, tear it down, break it down, and relegate it. They also remain uncertain about the people they have business relationship with. Their probability of trust with their business partners is lower than the average tolerance level. They will be the first to say "trust no one" but they want others to trust them. That cannot be, because it is not an equal minded situation.

BROKE LANE

Many people that we know are certified members of this lane. They complain of the inadequate pay that they get but do nothing about it. They blame the preacher for not praying hard enough. They get paid as little as it is but they fail to pay their tithes. They have forgotten what God says in the book of Haggai 1:6.

> *Ye have sown much, and bring in little; ye eat, but ye have not enough; ye drink, but ye are not filled with drink; ye clothe you, but there is none warm; and he that earns wages earns wages [to put it] into a bag with holes.*

The house of the Lord was in ruins but they failed to pay attention to it. They enriched their pockets but neglected the Most High God. Holes were in their pants' pockets; they wondered why they had no more money. They had ignored their Lord the Most High God! Everyone in the Broke Lane needs to search their hearts of what they do with their money. Broke Lane folks probably talked themselves into it. They confess without stopping how broke they are. Growing up, our elders used to tell us they were broke even when they were not only because they only didn't want to give us the money. They confessed it so much that they became broke indeed.

Those in the Broke Lane avoid wanting to give money and because of this, their confession become manifested. They are too broke to buy groceries, gasoline, give to church, even too broke to buy candy for the little kids. In trying to understand the characteristics of these broke individuals, I found that they have completely dissolved any trust of the system around them. They do not believe anyone can assist them in their financial debacle. They would rather cry broke in the morning, afternoon, and evening. To break this cycle of insufficiency, a person who believes that they are not making enough money should apply for a job where they can make more money. Talking about it is a mere use of words and it does not solve the problem. There needs to be action taken.

FEAR BOULEVARD

In this boulevard people allow past experiences to dictate what they do next. They remain in financial anxiety; they do not trust anyone with their money because they believe the person will rip them off. They are afraid to take chances; they inevitably will miss out on several opportunities to be great. Fear is a thief that must be contained. Apostle Paul writes to Timothy saying that the Lord has not given us the spirit of fear but of love, power and sound mind. As a thief, fear robs the individual the attempt to prosper. The individual looks at past experiences and fear grips their heart and makes them say, "I will pass on this one." As a result of fear, the destiny designed for a man is not achieved because they dare to dream big. On this particular boulevard it is needful to see that a truncated destiny is born from fear. A friend of mine that explored the possibility of making extra money through currency trading was discouraged because he lost money on his first try. He could not come back to trade again in the currency market because fear gripped his heart.

PAYCHECK CIRCLE

God help us all! In this street, everyone relies on receiving a paycheck from their employer. Truth be told, this street is the most important street in the lives of most readers. They rely solely on this check; everything around them does not matter. Why? This is because they believe that paycheck is their only source of true sufficiency. Most people would miss a midweek service for a paycheck. The other set of people will embrace this street like nothing else. They live practically for pay day. This means that they live to work. They constantly defend the slavery mentality of the employer. These are the ones in violation of Deuteronomy 8:18.

> *But thou shalt remember the LORD thy God: for [it is] he that giveth thee power to get wealth, that he may establish his covenant which he sware unto thy fathers, as [it is] this day.*

The works of your hands can only be blessed by God. The people at this location or street are receiving 35% of their blessing, let me prove it. If God says He would bless the works of your hands, then God blesses you with 100%; but if you work for someone else you are only getting a fractional blessing from the lord. Why?! Because 100% goes to Company ABC who you work for but ABC only pays you 35%.

The paycheck cycle means that you will live from paycheck to paycheck. Leaving no room for anything else, the bills cannot be paid well, at the end there is still deficit. You cannot even go to the movies; on the day you decide to go to the movie, you make your own popcorn and take with you. The person in the paycheck cycle is always unhappy about something. They are mad at their spouse, boss, organization and pastor. Why are they mad at the Pastor? They are mad at the pastor because he asks for tithes and offerings. Two years ago I was helping someone in this street to design their budget. I enquired about their tithes and offering. They were so upset with me that I would introduce that here, and so asked me to take tithes and offering away from their budget. Needless to tell you, we got that resolved because, bless be the name of the Lord, I am a Pastor. The cycle of paycheck to paycheck must be broken in the name of Jesus, Amen! As a new creation believer you are supposed to live in abundance according to John 10:10.

> *The thief cometh not, but for to steal, and to kill, and to destroy: I am come that they might have life and that they might have [it] more abundantly.*

Jesus said, "I have come to give you life and life more abundantly." The abundant life Jesus spoke of here covers the living from paycheck to paycheck. If you are a paycheck to paycheck cycle dweller, what if your job no longer exists? That is why we have to break the cycle of insufficiency.

LACK JUNCTION

This junction deals with the heart. It is a confession done with the mindset that I lack A, B and C. At the Lack Junction there is always a contention with what you do not have. There is no money to buy Johnny's shoes, clothes, and a cheeseburger. This particular street is very similar to the Broke Lane in that the dweller of this street complains about insufficiency like never before. In this street, there is a missing attribute - patience. There is a lack of patience in the Lack Junction. When the person in this street prays, they are more or less whining to God, saying: I can't pay for this or that. They forget that murmuring does nothing to please God. More than likely, they are in lack because of certain habits. The habits could include gambling, drinking, smoking, womanizing, shopping and partying. Then they wonder why they lack. When there is a known habit that compromises your account, lack becomes the outcome.

The theories discussed here are the ones that tend to pull us back and tear us down. Lack is no joke; a man or woman that lacks borrows or goes to borrow. The Bible says we should not borrow and because of their irresponsible borrowing habits, they now tend to expand lack. When they come across little money they try to pay off the interest of the loan that they borrowed and have not yet paid the principle. When they go shopping they shop for things that are outside their range only because they want to impress other people. They put themselves in bondage and cry out to the Lord. The Bible describes them in Psalms 107:27, *"They reel to and fro, and stagger like a drunken man, and are at their wits' end;"* they roll like a drunken sailor.

Lack happens also because they have disdained Gods' servant. The Psalmist says, *"He suffered no man to do them wrong: yea, he reproved kings for their sakes; [Saying], Touch not mine anointed, and do my prophets no harm"* (105:14-15). The moment a person on this street disdains the servant of the Most High God there comes an equal and opposite reaction to their callousness. So, beware!

Chapter 4
Challenges Caused by Insufficiency

Highlights

- Avoidable Ailments
- Family Conflict
- Lack of Accountability
- Creation of Unbelief System

A big aspect of insufficiency is the challenge it possess to those dealing with this condition. This challenge can ultimately create a hardship that is most uncomfortable for a person. In this chapter, we shall discuss four key areas that create challenges based on insufficiencies.

AVOIDABLE AILMENTS

Insufficiency is a disease that causes a chronic ailment. When someone is suffering from this condition the person tends to suffer from emotional set back. This puts the person in a very negative light. The person is consumed by excessive worries and as such the individual ends up with a health condition. Those that deal with insufficiency are apt to struggle with depression, oppression, suppression, regression, and temptation. They manifest all kinds of conditions that are bothersome to anyone in the natural. It is sufficed to say that they end up sometimes with an acute case of illness: stroke, high or low blood pressure, blood sugar, to mention a few. Insufficiency cannot be cured by drinking Tylenol or Advil, it is a condition that needs to be dealt with to avoid emotional catastrophe. There is no need to worry one's self into a health challenge. As of this writing, there is no known solution for the ailment that results from insufficiency.

Low self-esteem can be experienced when insufficiency rocks an individual. It creates a doubt in the self-esteem structure of that individual. This is because the person is unable to execute uncertain prior commitments. As such, the individual is unable to be successful in what they plan to do. Let us take a case a friend of mine who called me the other day as I was typing this portion of this book. The friend explained the excruciating pain surrounding their inability to do certain things they had planned. They told me they had several plans canceled because they could not afford those plans with their friend. They gave a vivid example of how they excused themselves from a trip to Italy. I can feel their pain and it is fair to say this dealt a blow to her self-esteem. She shared with me how embarrassed she was to tell anyone that she was in the Broke Lane. Praise God there is a testimony for her.

In 2009, I recall being severely broke and could not really pin point why. In retrospect, I can truly say the lack of reliable source of income is what led to it. I had just been disposed of three different houses that were rental properties. The tenants refused to pay, the mortgage company refused to cut me any slack, the bills continued piling up and one day a decision had to be made. You can imagine what happened! During this period it was very difficult to take the kids to buy ice cream; I would serve them a rationale to convince them that ice cream is not good for them because I faced complete lack. The streets discussed earlier are streets that I know so well, I have lived in these streets and have been delivered from them. I truly believe that your deliverance has come today. Amen!

Wherever you are reading this book, whether on the train, bus, or driving on a highway or the by-way (someone reading to you!) when you get to this point, I want you to shout a good Hallelujah!!!

FAMILY CONFLICT

Insufficiency is one source for family conflict. When there is insufficiency running in the family, tension tends to run high. The husband blames the wife for excessive spending of money and the wife blames him likewise. When insufficiency is the order in the family, it seems as if everyone is walking on egg shells. They are concerned, husband might be upset and the wife might be distressed. Whatever this situation is, no one seems happy. It is needful to add that a family with insufficiency rarely would do anything fun outside of the immediate family circles. They are either too concerned about how they would make ends meet or might be embarrassed that they cannot make ends meet. It really does not matter who cooperated with insufficiency to make the family to be suffering from insufficiency; what matters is the ability to get out of insufficiency. Many families have refused to do certain things together because of the embarrassing situations with insufficiency. When it is time to do something as a family, everybody's blood is boiling over. During birthday parties and other important family functions, families would opt out and ignore the relevance of such Kodak moments and thus fail to celebrate that goodness.

This threatens marriages and other meaningful relationships because every meaningful relationship or a marriage has trust built in it. The fiber of trust becomes a sharp point of discussion when there is constant argument surrounding insufficiency. The couple would innumerate how they have contributed to the success of the home; they are also quick to point accusatory fingers at one another. This must not be so. There appears to be an unwillingness to find the root cause of the problem due to the fact that each party is guilty of one thing or another. Their inability to find the root cause of insufficiency causes a deep problem. In some cases, the problem is swept under the rug and not addressed. Each problem discovered must be addressed and not swept under the rug. And this is my prayer in the name of Jesus Christ of Nazareth, Amen!

In these types of meaningful relationships, it is important to expel every selfish desire. So let us take for instance the case of Jack and Jill who are in a very meaningful relationship. They had a peculiar way of treating their assets. The assets that belonged to Jill were all Jill's. The assets that belonged to Jack were for both of them. As a Pastor, I would counsel that their assets should be equally owned by both of them without tangible or intangible separations. A further look into their relationship revealed that Jack was dealing with a bad habit of frequenting Las Vegas; as such Jill had no choice but to protect the interest of her money by saying that "my money belongs to me." For many years Jack was counseled to quit this financially harmful habit, but he resisted all forms of counseling and continued steadfastly. There must be an acceptable solution provided to Jill in order for her to allow her money to do things that would disengage the family from insufficiency. The overall story line is that a meaningful relationship should not focus on *what is yours is ours and what is mine is mine.* It is the most inappropriate way of handling a family problem (caution - This book is a financial help tool and not a marriage seminar tool. Please use appropriately).

LACK OF ACCOUNTABILITY

An in-depth analysis provides a good introspective outlook that shows that when one accepts responsibility or becomes more accountable, a solution can be attained regarding this subject of insufficiency. In the body of practical experience, an underlining theme shows that a person in the insufficiency dilemma is primarily responsible for being in that state. Therefore, it is prudent to say lack of accountability is a primary driver of insufficiency. Two key points come to mind to illustrate this theory.

Reliance on Others: Many people that find themselves in insufficiency have heavily relied on someone else as their entry point to sufficiency. The person they relied upon probably gave them money or money equivalent to solve certain problems. They have allowed their dependency to carry them far into a fantasy land and at the moment when their source is unable to support them anymore, their world is then shattered. Now that the helper is out of the picture, the person dealing with this condition is left exposed to the demons of insufficiency.

A lady once cried that our ministry failed to support her financially and that we put her in a financial bind. Folks, you be the judge… Our ministry would provide certain assistance to individuals that fellowshipped with us. We would help with their groceries and provide stipends to help with light or phone bills that are less than $100.00. When the financial position of the ministry was low, we were unable to continue to support the programs and even worse, people were not paying their tithes and offerings in order to replenish the program in which they were benefiting from… not only financially but spiritually.

Their attitude could almost be called ungratefulness because they professed that they could not sufficiently support the ministry financially. They did not stop there, they continued to speak badly about the ministry. Their attitude was worrisome, but we had to trust God. This type of mild disdain catches God's attention. God is clearly unhappy about the fact that His ministry is disdained by the people. Then these people wonder why they are still in a place of lack or insufficiency. Note that they have disdained the work of God; they have casted down the man of God, and they have used evil tongue in speaking against providence provision of the Most High God; the Psalmist decried this type behavior (105:14-15).

He suffered no man to do them wrong: yea, he reproved kings for their sakes; [Saying], Touch not mine anointed, and do my prophets no harm.

Excessive Spending Habit: The second point relating to lack of accountability pertains to a person mired in bondage, a cycle, or a cage of doing something excessively without control or discretion. The person perpetrates evil towards money! Everything they do is all about them; they want more clothes, shoes, cars, homes. Simply put, they desire excessively more of every worldly thing, rather than more of Jesus. They may give lip service to the song "I want more of you Jesus" but God knows the heart. They are the ones that will not stay more than one hour in Bible study; they are impatient, intolerant, and inconsiderate. When you ask them to do the works of God they will either reject your request, or find a very lame excuse why it is not necessary to do it. These are the ones that are not accountable for anything. When their well runs dry, they blame everything (their shoes to their clothing) and everyone from the pastor to their so-called enemies; there is no time when they accept responsibility or accountability for anything. These are the ones needing true deliverance (not judging, but just telling the truth!).

If you dig deeper you will find their agenda is contrary to the ministry's agenda and God's agenda; and then they wonder – Why!!!

When the Pastor gives instruction or provides sound counseling in an area of struggle, they hiss and snap their fingers; then they shake their heads in disagreement, unbelief, or disgust. They dump and dislodge the instruction when they are exiting the premises. Then they pick up the telephone and call their friends to gossip about the instruction given by the man of God, saying that the man of God's counsel was unwise. These characteristics confirm the attitude of people that Asaph talked about in Psalms 78:41, *"Yea, they turned back and tempted God, and limited the Holy One of Israel."*

These individuals disbelieve God and disobey what God ministers to them. They also do not trust God; they have forgotten all that the Lord has done for them, even in the days when nothing seemed to have worked. In their hearts they had been insincere with God; when they pray, they don't even believe in their own prayers and go through a religious manifestation of their prayers. No revelation of the words they pray, yet they wonder why… I must declare deliverance is needed. The church elders should ask directly – "Who needs to be delivered from insufficiency?"

CREATION OF AN UNBELIEF SYSTEM

By the mere fact that there is the issue of insufficiency, those that are involved may find themselves struggling and creating a new avenue for unbelief. Unbelief is when faith and hope receive strangulation. When a person is dealing in unbelief and in some cases disbelief, it is almost impossible to shed light on their condition. This is because they only believe in the gross darkness of their situation

> *For, behold, the darkness shall cover the earth, and gross darkness the people* (Isaiah 60:2).

Why is this? This is as a result of what they only know. They cannot spend as they want and cannot save as they want and they consistently pinch nickels and dimes. It creates room for unbelief. Clearly, my reader is a Christian; but when insufficiency strikes hard, the Christianity seems to turn weak immediately. This unbelief system is clearly contrary to the Word of God. The book of Hebrews 11:6 puts this way:

> *But without faith [it is] impossible to please [him]: for he that cometh to God must believe that he is, and [that] he is a rewarder of them that diligently seek him.*

By this pronouncement from God, it is clear that those dealing with insufficiency are not properly aligning themselves with God, because our God is a God of abundance! We have a very BIG God who has given us grace to overcome insufficiency, that is why He said, *"My grace is sufficient for you"* (2 Corinthians 12:9), and the complete verse reads:

> *And he said unto me, My grace is sufficient for thee: for my strength is made perfect in weakness. Most gladly therefore will I rather glory in my infirmities, that the power of Christ may rest upon me.*

Chapter 5
Solution I: Intangible

Highlights

- Do Not Forsake God
- Watch Self-Reliance
- Avoid Erroneous Situations

The conceptual solution for insufficiency is to allow God to control the total essence of your financial disposition. Breaking the cycle of insufficiency is really a challenge that must be addressed forcefully in order for those trapped in this web to be set free and completely liberated. In the natural, this condition needs a practical solution in order to satisfy the conditions of need or want. Too many people settle in the mess and as such, they have taken this as a norm. There is nothing normal about living in insufficiency. It is actually abnormal to live a life like that. A person living this life has been deprived of God's best. That's why a solution must be suggested in this book.

The title of this book deals with a practical remedy to a serious situation. Take for instance, a person living in this cycle of insufficiency. This person would pray, fast, and give their last dime - yet, there appears to be a lack of solution. The person's situation becomes gravitationally dire. Psalmist Asaph confronted the same situation in Psalm 73. He watched nonbelievers prosper. He knew them and he knew their belief system; amazingly he knew they never missed a beat as they prospered very well. Personally, he knew something was off, but could not place his finger on the real deal. He writes in Psalm 73:2-3.

But as for me, my feet were almost gone; my steps had well-nigh slipped...For I was envious at the foolish, [when] I saw the prosperity of the wicked.

He knew that God is a Just God; he knew that God is good. He knew all the adjectives ascribed to God - faithful, kind, gentle, provider, protector, awesome, etc. These adjectives remained intact for Asaph. Something happened during his spiritual journey. The enemy pushed his button so much that in Psalm 73:16-17 he writes:

> *When I thought to know this, it [was] too painful for me; until I went into the sanctuary of God; [then] understood I their end.*

If he had slipped, this could have cost him dearly. However, the house of God brought him peace and comfort and a reminder of God's graciousness. The sanctuary served as his place of refuge and reassurance. This story brings into focus the theme of this book. A moment in which we ask God a simple question called "Why."

I have provided a few practical examples that would help people in this conundrum break out of this mess and to live a life designed by God. I believe that the solutions provided below would help my reader in solving the problem. In all cases, see the good and the practicality. Please avoid criticizing the solution because it may not apply to you, but someone else might find it very impactful. Enjoy the solution.

DO NOT FORSAKE GOD

It appears that many people dealing with the problem of insufficiency have had a tendency to forsake God. They have in one way or another stopped from fellowshipping with God; many times they tend to cage God and have not really accepted the expression of God to take dominion or authority in their life. My reader might ask, "How can you forsake God?" Thanks for asking, here are some ways in which God has been forsaken:

- Ignoring actual prayer times with God.

- Failing to include God in your decision making process.

- Playing games with and not being sincere with Him.

- Refusing to read His Word, to follow instructions He might have given you.

- Being consumed with self-centered agenda.

- Not fellowshipping with the saints, ignoring the saints for whatever reason.

All of these points amount to forsaking God. In light of this, Jeremiah 2:13 states:

> *For my people have committed two evils; they have forsaken me the fountain of living waters, [and] hewed them out cisterns, broken cisterns, that can hold no water.*

Due to the fact that you chose to follow your own path, you have failed to see the value of fellowshipping with your Maker. As a result of your refusal to commune with Him, He might have allowed the cycle of insufficiency so that you can find your way back to Him. Anytime you remove God from the equation, you find yourself depending on your own strength. Your strength is functionally inadequate. You and I need God's help to boost the strength we have. Many corporate executives may not be very vocal and expressive about their beliefs openly; arguably, some believe in God and so they pray more frequently than we know about. They seek God's counsel. They are smart to believe and follow God. They are not careless with God.

WATCH SELF-RELIANCE

One of the most dangerous things a man could do to one's self is to openly confess self-reliance on anything. Those who are self-reliant become consumed by the process they have designed. A self-reliant person has little or no value or reverence for God. In their hearts, they believe that they can do it without God or anyone's help. In view of this, Psalm 14 says *"The fool hath said in his heart, [There is] no God."*

A fool is the person that convinces herself that there is no need for God and that they can go through life in their own abilities and capabilities. In 1841, Ralph Waldo Emerson pushed the idea of self-reliance and presented certain characteristics. According to Marinova and Hossain (2006), "Emerson in a similarly titled essay published in 1841 which stressed the trust in one's present thoughts, skills, originality, belief in own capabilities and genius and living from within" (p. 2).

As impressive as self-reliance can be, there are dangers associated with it. In discussing The Danger of Self-Reliance, Darryl Dash provided a touching story in Darryl's blog on January 17, 2010, stating:

"Jack Miller was a pastor in Philadelphia. In 1970, Miller resigned from his church and seminary. Neither the church members nor the seminary students were changing in the ways that he had hoped. He didn't know how to help them, so he quit and spent weeks too depressed to do anything but cry.

He came to realize a couple of things:

- That he was motivated by personal glory and the approval of people, rather than being motivated only by God's glory.

- That he had been trusting in his own abilities, rather than in the promises God had made and the power of the Holy Spirit.

A turning point came when he realized his motivation for ministry had been all wrong, and that he had been relying on the wrong person to do ministry - himself. He came to understand that the work of ministry was far too big for him to accomplish on his own strength. He came to understand that it was his pride and self-reliance that was keeping him from having a significant part in this great work of Christ...He saw that doing Christ's work in Christ's way meant giving up all dependence on himself, acknowledging how poor in spirit he was, and then relying exclusively on Jesus for His grace.

He withdrew his resignation, and he changed. From that point on his ministry was characterized by the themes of humility, vital faith, and constant prayer. He found that he grew as he admitted every day that he was a desperate sinner in constant need of the grace of God. He believed that doing Christ's work in Christ's way is impossible using human resources; we must be connected to Christ through prayer. His ministry accomplished more than he could have thought once he got to the point of humble dependence instead of self-reliance.

Friends, we are continually faced with situations in ministry that are greater than we can handle. Nevertheless, we have a tendency to be *self-reliant* instead of *God-reliant*. God calls us to repent and depend on Him. Anything else is idolatry" (Dash, 2010).

A self-design solution which effectively does not have God in it is doomed to face life challenges and would be insufficient in all regards. In some cases there will be short term benefits, but as time goes by, the short term benefits wear away.

AVOID ERRONEOUS SITUATIONS

In many cases we fail to deal with certain peculiar errors of life. Unless these errors are addressed, one might remain in a stagnant condition over a lengthy period of time. Errors of life are man instigated. They occurred as a result of poor judgment and inadequate resolution of certain circumstances. Some are:

- For instance, a Christian that is affiliated with a church that has no regard for true spiritual values but only deals with religious values would find himself or herself in poor understanding of God's standards.

- There are instances whereby the person can simply not control the language spoken by confessing wrongly or negatively. The person might be confessing death instead of life into a particular situation.

- There might be the case of not believing that God has not given us the spirit of fear, as such everything the person does is riddled in fear and not in the confidence of God's power.

- The simple use of "In the name of Jesus" can be effective and can eliminate error in one's life. The reason for the effective prayer in using "In the name of Jesus Christ" is because you have invited Jesus Christ to the decision making table. And when Jesus Christ helps you with making a decision, errors literally disappear.

- The mistakes of life are a continuing lie perpetrated by the devil. The lie appears so real until one starts to believe the lie. When the lie is believed, then the person would act on that lie, which in turn creates an error.

- Life's errors precipitated the wisest King ever to acknowledge this issue in the book of Ecclesiastics 10:5-7, *"There is an evil [which] I have seen under the sun, as an error [which] proceedeth from the ruler: Folly is set in great dignity, and the rich sit in low place. I have seen servants upon horses, and princes walking as servants upon the earth."*

In a real sense, after your college education, you should be gainfully employed. Your professional qualifications and candidacy should never be questioned, but this is not the case. Instead, the company has failed to hire you and when you are hired, you are paid an amount less than the going rate. It is an error! You rule! God has given that to you when you were created. He told you to walk in dominion, *"And God blessed them, and God said unto them, Be fruitful, and multiply, and replenish the earth, and subdue it: and have dominion over the fish of the sea, and over the fowl of the air, and over every living thing that moveth upon the earth"* (Genesis 1:28).

However, you have allowed the enemy to trick you into believing that a paycheck to paycheck life is just as good as anything else.

- There are many people not as anointed as you, but they ride the Word of God without apology. They get their breakthroughs and try their best to avoid the errors of life. As you know, in many cases, the errors committed have held folks back. A prophetic word spoken on them does not seem to have room for expression. This must not be.

- In some homes because the husband lost his job, the wife makes nonsense of him. She now runs the home and dictates to the husband what should be done in that home. It is an error.

The cure for this error is serious intercessory prayers and special deliverance sessions. Error is not our portion; therefore we must not grant it permission into our homes and checkbooks.

Chapter 6
Solution II:
Raising Capital (Part 1)

Highlights

- Love Letter from God
- Personal Income

LOVE LETTER FROM GOD

Over the past chapters, we have been discussing the elements and ills of insufficiency. It has become crystal clear that there needs to be an adequate capitalization in order to defeat the demons surrounding insufficiency. Please note that the solutions proposed so far are absolutely germane for breaking the evil cycle of insufficiency. As a result, it is needful for us to understand the various ways by which capitalization can be achieved. Please note that in all cases there is a need for some groundwork. Whatever the case may be, it is your responsibility to ensure that money comes into your hands.

There are certain broad principles to keep in mind when discussing capitalization. The first principle is for you to answer the question "Why are you in business?" It may be that your calling is not to start a business. If that is the case, you might be called to do something else. To be insufficiently funded can create challenges for your business or your personal life. For this sake, you sincerely need to answer the question of whether you need more capital or not. You also need to answer what you need the capital for. As for you (the reader), you will need to determine if there is a true need for the capital or not. A direct question is "Why do I need more money?" The second principle to this insufficiency drama is to become declarative and say, you need to make money. Many times we are erroneously relaxed by insufficient capitalization; we therefore, rely on the little we have. We find ourselves squeezing the heck out of the little dollar. But excuse me, our God is big! Our God is able! Our God is rich! You cannot use one dollar to buy everything. Ask Him and He will make the provision for you, therefore, go ahead and make money!

The third principle, in this capitalization debate is to make a difference. You have been called to make a difference but due to insufficiency you have ignored making a difference. You consistently complain about not having enough and because of this you have not impacted your generation. The Bible said David had to impact his generation without which he could not die.

For David, after he had served his own generation by the will of God, fell on sleep, and was laid unto his fathers, and saw corruption (Acts 13:36).

David had to serve his generation despite the challenges he was faced with. There were many times that King Saul sought to kill David but was unsuccessful. The reason why he was unsuccessful was because David was required to serve his generation. The fourth principle surrounding capital deficiency is to satisfy God's purpose for you. God has uniquely and specifically designed you for a purpose. You have been singularly called and chosen to solve a problem in this generation. When you were formed you were targeted to resolve a complicated circumstance in your time.

That's why God told Jeremiah that:

> *Before I formed thee in the belly I knew thee; and before thou camest forth out of the womb I sanctified thee, [and] I ordained thee a prophet unto the nations* (Jeremiah 1:5).

The prophet was uniquely assigned to lament and intercede over the circumstance in Israel. He was called to be a prophet to the nation. Jeremiah's approach to receive a word from God gave birth to a love letter that was written to the children of Israel in exile. For a refresher, here are portions of the letter (Jeremiah 29:1-14) once more and again.

> *Now these are the words of the letter that Jeremiah the prophet sent from Jerusalem to the remainder of the elders who were carried away captive—to the priests, the prophets, and all the people whom Nebuchadnezzar had carried away captive from Jerusalem to Babylon. ² (This happened after Jeconiah the king, the queen mother, the eunuchs, the princes of Judah and Jerusalem, the craftsmen, and the smiths had departed from Jerusalem.) ³ The letter was sent by the hand of Elasah the son of Shaphan, and Gemariah the son of Hilkiah, whom Zedekiah king of Judah sent to Babylon, to Nebuchadnezzar king of Babylon, saying, ⁴ Thus says the LORD of hosts, the God of Israel, to all who were carried away captive, whom I have caused to be carried away from Jerusalem to Babylon. ⁵Build houses and dwell in them; plant gardens and eat their fruit. ⁶Take wives and beget sons and daughters;*

and take wives for your sons and give your daughters to husbands, so that they may bear sons and daughters— that you may be increased there, and not diminished. [7]And seek the peace of the city where I have caused you to be carried away captive, and pray to the LORD for it; for in its peace you will have peace. [8]For thus says the LORD of hosts, the God of Israel: Do not let your prophets and your diviners who are in your midst deceive you, nor listen to your dreams which you cause to be dreamed. [9]For they prophesy falsely to you in My name; I have not sent them, says the LORD. [10]For thus says the LORD: After seventy years are completed at Babylon, I will visit you and perform My good word toward you, and cause you to return to this place. [11]For I know the thoughts that I think toward you, says the LORD, thoughts of peace and not of evil, to give you a future and a hope. [12]Then you will call upon Me and go and pray to Me, and I will listen to you. [13]And you will seek Me and find Me, when you search for Me with all your heart. [14]I will be found by you, says the LORD, and I will bring you back from your captivity; I will gather you from all the nations and from all the places where I have driven you, says the LORD, and I will bring you to the place from which I cause you to be carried away captive."

This love letter from God was written to encourage those who have been exiled from their place of wealth. These are those who have inadvertently held on to insufficiency. I truly believe that you have been encouraged by the words of this love letter to you.

Thanks be to the Most High God for such love…

God has spoken and has released a word into the situation. He used verse 11 to stress His love to us *"For I know the thoughts that I think toward you, says the LORD, thoughts of peace and not of evil, to give you a future and a hope."* It is clear that God is not pleased that some of us are constantly in a state of insufficiency. God's purpose for us must be fulfilled, you can no longer be engaged in the drama of insufficiency. You should be a person in quest for success because success is your heritage. This is only possible when you are aligning yourself with God. In your day to day operation, are you being intertwined with the Holy Spirit, so:

> … *thine ears shall hear a word behind thee, saying, this [is] the way, walk ye in it, when ye turn to the right hand, and when ye turn to the left* (Isaiah 30:21).

When you hear from the Holy Spirit to go to the left or to the right, it is a sign of care, compassion, and courage for you. The assignment of the Holy Spirit is too great and more perfect than your GPS. So, when the little voice says, go to the left or right, it is for a purpose.

The other day, a businessman informed me of a unique encounter with the Holy Spirit. This businessman who was serving as a currency consultant believed that he heard the Holy Spirit whisper to him that the Japanese Yen was weakening against the US dollar and other major currencies. On the day of our discussion the US dollar versus the Japanese yen was at 92.5, the businessman did not do anything, meaning he failed to act on the tip from the Holy Spirit. He did not act upon the instruction of the Holy Spirit because he probably wanted the Holy Spirit to sit with him and discuss 'blah-blah-blah' on the situation. The Holy Spirit is a gentle Spirit, He gives instructions mostly softly and then moves on; and then it is up to us to act upon the instructions. At approximately 7pm Chicago time, the USD/JPY (US dollar to Japanese Yen exchange rate) saw a 600 pip move; the Japanese Yen depreciated by 600 points within the hour of the instruction from the Holy Spirit. Apparently, the new Finance Minister announced that there was need to stress the Yen, in order to flood Japanese economy with moderately cheap products.

Well, the Holy Spirit knew the announcement was going to happen within the hour in which He gave instructions to the businessman. The businessman was lamenting and saying to me that he had missed the boat. On this day alone, according to him when I did the analysis this businessman could have made a $600,000 profit. This profit could have helped with satisfying God's purpose for him even in a short time. God is particular about the things that concern us. He is not willing to mortgage our purpose for anything else. As covenanted children, we need to trust God more. The Psalmist says His interest in us provoked Him to include Psalms 138:8 in the Bible.

The LORD will perfect [that which] concerneth me: thy mercy, O LORD, [endureth] forever: forsake not the works of thine own hands.

Several ways of raising capital has been identified for you, the reader. The way to look at this capitalization process is to differentiate them as in how they contribute to your pool of cash (the sources are income you personally contribute); the gifts you receive from others; any short-term borrowing from others, and other basic avenues.

PERSONAL INCOME

The first source of raising money is through the works of your hands. This is the most gratifying means of income because it does not tie any form of obligation to the income. Instead, the work you have done is being rewarded.

(1) Wages and Salaries: This is the money earned from working for a company or private employer. This money only represents the amount of hours (if hourly employed or salary employed) your employer makes sure that you are paid remuneration each month either bi-weekly or bi-monthly, or weekly. The key point here is for you to raise cash to pay your bills or do other things. In any case, a job is needed to help sustain your expenditures either through others employing you or to be self-employed.

(2) Private Savings Account: I know of some people who would automatically send monies to their private bank account on every paycheck they get, it is a discipline that is necessary. They send their money without any cause. They don't even miss the money because they have adjusted to not seeing that portion of their paycheck anymore. We all need to have a private bank account.

(3) Favorable Budgetary Circumstances: When you budget as discussed and because you might have some favorability in your budget computation, you stand a chance of gaining some cash for spending. This is more common than rare. For instance, if your budgeted income is $100,000 and your budgeted expenses equal $99,000, then the income over the expense would by $1,000. Assuming at the end of the budget period the income realized is $105,000 and the actual expenses incurred were $90,000; this would create a favorable budget circumstance of $14,000. The variance $14,000 would now become the extra cash that you have raised during the budget period. Very impressive!

(4) Rental Income: The fall of the housing market has created a new breed of wealthy individuals. These are the ones that were able to purchase real estate at scrap value and foreclosure rates. They were able to renovate the property and make them available for rent. Rental income is a reliable source of income when there are stable tenants. Some tenants are a bit challenging to deal with, they refuse to pay and will grieve the owner of the property. Rental income can be that income that pays off the mortgage if any mortgage still exists in the property. The rental income does not automatically serve as a tax liability because of the use of limited liability company (LLC) provisions. A lot of people shield their income through the LLC to avoid unnecessary tax consequences. Rental income can also be in the form of renting out personal property such as a boat, vacation home, jewelry, car, finished basements and parking space.

(5) Government Entitlements: This government's privilege is a system that is designed to help its people in time of need. Here's a brief history for you, between 2008 and 2012 the US government and the world economy faced a drastic recession, which caused many people to lose their jobs, many homes to be foreclosed upon, many cars to be repossessed, many families to suffer set-backs; many organizations to be shut down and etc. The stories were not good at all! It was a time we needed the government's assistance and intervention. The unemployment office is one of the branches at the state level. This office is designed to assist you when you are unemployed. It is unwise not to go and receive what is due to you. Remember that you paid into the unemployment insurance account while you were employed. On the day that you are no longer employed, it is important for you to visit the unemployment office to claim your entitlement. It is not much money that is given but it is better than nothing. There are other state wide and federal government assistant programs that can be beneficial, such as public aid, food stamps (link cards) and government insurance. Too many people criticize these government support programs because of one reason or another. I am not justifying or rejecting it, but saying that it is a source of help that needs to be genuinely used for its purpose. What you receive from the government should not to be used to purchase alcohol, cigarettes or drugs but for the intended purpose - food!

(6) Pension Plan: You are encouraged to become a part of the pension system whereby at a stipulated age you can draw down your pension and you do not have to worry about what happens when you retire from the company. You will receive a steady stream of income.

Chapter 7
Solution II:
Raising Capital (Part 2)

Highlights

- Gifts
- Borrowing
- Investments & Other Ways

GIFTS

Raising capital through the generosity of others and others believing in you is called gifting. Giving a gift is a conscious decision to support the agenda and aspirations of the person receiving the gift. The person given has a true trust and a conviction that the support is necessary. Below are a few ways in which giving is executed and cherished by the receiver.

(7) Inheritance: This relates to when a person receives money or money equivalent that they did not work for from a wealthy estate. The inheritance account could be very buoyant and could have a lot of good provisions. In many cases, there is cash involved that can solve immediate insufficiency needs. There are many people who get their inheritance gift through the passing of a family member or friend. Although this is not very common, it is a source that can transform the capitalization structure of a person. In the American story culture there are a few families that have bequeathed inheritances to generations down, the stories of the Kennedys, Rockefellers, Waltons, and so on. This is even supported by the scriptures.

A good [man] leaveth an inheritance to his children's children: and the wealth of the sinner [is] laid up for the just (Proverbs 13:22).

(8) Wealthy Family Member: There are several families whereby certain family members are doing very well for themselves. These family members have had the pleasure and blessing to become very wealthy. They can serve as a source of capital. They normally will set aside monies for family members in need. In reality, they are really philanthropic in nature. They care about family and because of that, they provide the necessary capitalization to ambitious family members. Their gift to the family member is really an investment to that person. There is an emotional connection that surfaces any time this is looked upon. They just don't throw money into the situation, instead they ask the family member to present a proposal for help. Inevitably, a lump sum of cash or cash equivalent is received in this process. The wealthy family member can be an uncle who has a true love for his family members. In this case, an ambitious nephew, niece or a cousin could be a beneficiary of this gift.

(9) Someone Sows into Your Life: This is more common than we give credit for. There are several individuals who would sow into your life because they truly believe in you. They also believe in your calling as a minister of the Most High God. Every now and then, someone would call and ask for your bank account information so that they can be a blessing to you. As a pastor I have received these types of calls and offers to bless me, praise be to God for His blessings. A young man shared with me a testimony about two years ago; he told me that one of the elders of the church called him to say that the Lord asked to bless him. The young man opened up the envelope and saw a $1,000 check. That was such an encouraging blessing. When the young man asked the elder why, he indicated that God was tugging in his heart and asked him to bless this young man. God can release sowers into our lives. Normally, this type of gift is financial in nature and available to be spent, to deal with insufficiency.

(10) Scholarships and Grants: This source of capital helps a student or someone undertaking a particular venture to fund the task. There are several organizations and individual endowments that offer free giving towards a venture. When I was in school, I received several scholarships to help fund my education. I applied to the United Negro College fund and also applied to a diverse pool of funds. The Lord blessed me, and my college education was paid for. In my book, *Financial Maturity after the Recession*, I stated " the following is a list of scholarships and their Web addresses to pass along to friends and family members with college-bound kids so that this free money will not go to waste."

	Scholarships	Website
1	Bell Labs Fellowships for under-represented minorities	www.bell-labs.com/
2	Student Inventors Scholarships	www.invent.org/ collegiate/

3	Student Video Scholarships	www.christophers.org/vidcon2k.html
4	Coca-Cola Two-Year College Scholarships	www.coca-colascholars.org/programs.html
5	Holocaust Remembrance Scholarships	www.holocaust.hklaw.com/
6	Ayn Rand Essay Scholarships	www.aynrand.org/contests/
7	Brand Essay Competition	www.institutefor-brandleadership.org/IBLEssayContest-2002Rules.htm
8	Gates Millennium Scholarships	www.gmsp.org/nominationmaterials/read.dbm?ID=12
9	Xerox Scholarships for Students	www2.xerox.com/go/xrx/about_xerox/about_xerox_detail.jsp
10	Sports Scholarships and Internships	www.ncaa.org/about/scholarships.html
11	National Association of Black Journalists Scholarships (NABJ)	www.nabj.org/html/studentsvcs.html
12	Saul T. Wilson Scholarships (Veterinary)	www.aphis.usda.gov/mb/mrphr/jobs/stw.html
13	Thurgood Marshall Scholarship Fund	www.thurgoodmarshall-fund.org/sk_v6.cfm

14	Fin Aid: The Smart Students Guide to Financial Aid	www.finaid.org < http:// www.finaid.org/>
15	Presidential Freedom Scholarships	www.nationalservice. org/scholarships/
16	Microsoft Scholarship Program	www.microsoft.com/ college/ scholarships/minority. asp
17	Wired Scholar Free Scholarship Search	www.wiredscholar.com/ paying/ scholarship_search/ pay_scholarship_se
18	Hope Scholarships & Lifetime Credits	www.ed.gov/inits/ hope/
19	William Randolph Hearst Endowed Scholarship for Minority Students	www.apsanet.org/PS/ grants/aspen3.cfm
20	Multiple List of Minority Scholarships	www.gehon.ir.miami. edu/financial- assistance/ Scholarship/black.html
21	Guaranteed Scholarships	www.guaranteed- scholarships.com/
22	Boeing scholarships	www.boeing.com/ companyoffices/ educationrelations/ scholarships
23	Easley National Scholarship Program	www.naas.org/senior. htm

24	Maryland Artists Scholarships	www.maef.org/
25	Jacki Tuckfield Memorial Graduate Business Scholarship for AfrAm students in S. Florida)	www.jackituckfield.org/
26	Historically Black College & University Scholarships	www.iesabroad.org/ info/hbcu.htm
27	Actuarial Scholarships for Minority Students	www.beanactuary.org/ minority/ scholarships.htm
28	International Students Scholarships & Aid Help	www.iefa.org/
29	INROADS internships	www.inroads.org/
30	ACT-SO "Olympics of the Mind" Scholarships	www.naacp.org/work/ actso/act-so.shtml
31	Black Alliance for Educational Options Scholarships	www.baeo.org/options/ privatelyfinanced.jsp
32	Siemens Foundation Competition	www.siemens-foundation.org/

This list is needed to start trying to track down funding for your education or venture. Please let me caution that if one door closes, there is another door that opens. Do not be discouraged if you are unable to get money from the top five on this list but note that the next tier of organizations might be willing to give you money. Two years ago, I was mentoring a particular MBA candidate. We did a project in which we looked up addresses for one hundred organizations. We wrote a letter asking for funding for an MBA program and sent them to all 100 companies. There were some that took interest in our approach to get funding and then there were some that could not provide the assistance. The moral of this story is that there is a need to creatively assess funds from these organizations. The other day a small business owner and I sat down to investigate ways to raise capital. We searched the internet to obtain foundations, endowments, philanthropists, and charities. We sent letters to over 55 of them. The responses were absolutely encouraging!

According to Wikipedia (2013), "The Bill & Melinda Gates Foundation (B&MGF or the Gates Foundation) is the largest transparently operated private foundation in the world, founded by Bill and Melinda Gates. It is "driven by the interests and passions of the Gates family." The primary aims of the foundation are, globally, to enhance healthcare and reduce extreme poverty, and in America, to expand educational opportunities and access to information technology. The foundation, based in Seattle, Washington, is controlled by its three trustees: Bill Gates, Melinda Gates and Warren Buffett. Other principal officers include Co-Chair William H. Gates, Sr. and Chief Executive Officer Jeff Raikes.

It had an endowment of US$36.2 billion as of September 30, 2012. The scale of the foundation and the way it seeks to apply business techniques to giving makes it one of the leaders in the philanthropic-capitalism revolution in global philanthropy, though the foundation itself notes that the philanthropic role has limitations. In 2007, its founders were ranked as the second most generous philanthropists in America. A 2013 Bloomberg report stated that, as of May 16, 2013, Bill Gates had donated US$28 billion to the foundation."

BORROWING

Another source of capital is called borrowing. Although borrowing is not an ideal way but it serves as a means to an end. There are many implications surrounding borrowing. Many financial advisors would counsel against borrowing even the Bible says we should owe no man (Romans 13:8). So it is important that the following principles be reviewed carefully before attempting to borrow. The borrower must assess if the money is truly needed. There are moments when the money to be borrowed is not needed but due to the fact that the person has a connection to the borrowing facility they may then go for the loan. The amount borrowed must be commensurate to your equity.

For instance, a person with a total income of $100,000 should only be extended credit facility of $50,000. Recently, most people have found themselves being over extended in debt. They cannot pay their bills, accommodate their leisure needs because there is no money, unable to give money to others, all because they are completely extended. A borrower should honestly take into consideration that the loan must be liquidated within a 36 month period or shorter. The idea is to get the individuals out of debt. The Bible says you ought to be the lender and not the borrower. Due to the stress with borrowing, most people find themselves filing for bankruptcy. This is not good. Although people can argue in favor of the benefits, it still stands as an irresponsible means of resolving your debt crises. Where bankruptcy is involved, the borrower is relieved of the loan but not the consequences, owing to the fact the seven years of your life will have a tarnished credit rating. Therefore, do not take a loan that you hope the government will relieve you from.

(11) Loans through Financial Institutions: These are commercial loans that financial institutions grant to individuals or businesses. These loans normally require certain conditions from the financial institution. The financial institution might ask for a budget, current financial statements (which should include a balance sheet, income statement, and a cash flow analysis). Very importantly the financial institution looks at your credit worthiness. An analysis of these items could provide a basis for your loan to be approved or denied. The financial institutions are very careful granting loans since the recession. During the recession, several bankruptcies were noted and several delinquencies were found to be common. The financial institution has a formula to determine your ability to repay the loan granted to you. They also want to keep a relationship with you as a customer.

(12) Family & Friends: These loans from family and friends are truly good for one key reason, they do not reflect on your credit report. These are loans that you approach a family or friend for, you ask for a certain amount of money with a promise to pay them back in the future. In some cases these people could charge you a certain percentage of interest or could say to you to just return the same amount loaned. This type of loan is granted because of certain hardships or because there is a venture a family or friend believes in that you are undertaking. The key down side to this loan is that personal relationships could be affected especially if the payment is not made as agreed upon. The other angle of potential challenges are if the parties involved start to feud over other issues not relating to the loan.

An example of this happens to be when there is a disagreement between both parties over an unrelated matter; both individuals could play a harsh role whereby the lender will demand for the money back or the borrower refusing to pay back. The conclusion of this matter is both parties should be careful when going into this arrangement with a family or friend. While this type of loan security is convenient it can be very risky too because the borrower might honestly not have the money to repay. There are several stories of this type of borrowing. Jane borrowed from Sarah $1,250 for her rent because she was just laid off and she promised Sarah when she received her severance package she would pay the loan back. However, when it was time to pay the money, Jane could not repay Sarah because of many other outstanding obligations. It is needless to tell you how this ended.

(13) Saving Account - 401k: Of all types of borrowing, this could arguably be the best form of money to be borrowed. This is a loan from you to you. This loan is when you choose to borrow from your retirement account. In borrowing from you, there are a few things that would happen before the process is over.

- You have to have an adequate funded retirement account.

- Your money in the 401k account should still reside with the financial institution through the organization.

- Because of statutory requirements the 401k money cannot be toyed with. As a result, the money can only be accessed through hardship and or loan. When it is hardship money you are accessed a 10% penalty for early withdrawal. It is considered early withdrawal if you are less than 59 1/2 years old.

- When trying to secure hardship money, there are

several requirements and documentation requested by your organization. Please note that this 401k money is considered retirement money and so the organization would make it difficult to withdraw the money. As a loan provision, it is crafted in a way whereby only 50% of the money can be withdrawn. Also, the loan amount to be repaid is factored into your paycheck. It is difficult to not repay this loan. Even as you pay back, the loan interest is factored in at the point the loan was originated.

(14) Credit Card Account: When you read different financial consultancy books and when you listen to different consultants, you will hear them say that you should not use credit cards. It is all true; however, the credit card is a source of financing. When a bank issues you a credit card with a huge line of credit, you could use portions of the credit card to complete some of your transactions as needed. Note that it is called credit and would have to be paid off at the end of the month before interest expense will start to accrue. Unpaid credit balances normally will have hefty interest rates attached to them. Using a credit card to conduct business signifies that there is a particular sum of income expected to liquidate what has been borrowed.

(15) Home Equity Line of Credit: This type of capitalization is when you borrow from the equity in your home. The equity in your home is determined by deducting the amount you owe on the home from the value of the home. Financial institutions jump at the opportunity to loan borrowers' money through this avenue. Why is that the case? Because the equity is collateralized by the property; therefore, the financial institutions can almost not lose in borrowing to you. Monies from equity line of credit are normally used to enhance or improve the home, start a business, and pay off huge debts. Since the interest from credit cards are not deductible except for business organizations, what people do is that they use their equity line of credit to pay off huge credit card bills. Using an equity line of credit has a great advantage during tax filing. The IRS allows the borrower to deduct interest expense from the equity line of credit.

(16) Governmental Loans: These loans are absolutely the best to get because of all the benefits that they carry.

- They carry very low and reasonable interest rates. The interest rate on a loan determines how big or small the repayment would be. Normally, the interest on commercial loans could be ridiculously high especially when the borrower is dealing with credit dilemmas.

- Governmental loans are generally more lenient to obtain or to receive than commercial loans. Governmental loans serve as a basis to help the disenfranchised and the ambitious.

During the 2013 storms that raged through the Middle

America, people and businesses lost their possessions and personal effects as a result of the storm. The government stepped in to assist these people to rebuild their communities, their homes and businesses. Governmental loans specifically target certain areas of life such as student loans, small business administration loan and the veterans benefit loan. The federal government helps to underwrite some housing loans. The department of housing and urban development is responsible for enforcing all fair housing conditions. Whereas, the FHA (Federal Housing Administration) insured loan is a mortgage insurance that covers specific approved lenders. The potential area of challenges in trying to secure government loans are:

(I)   The forms are tedious and can be very intrusive.

(II)   They require very much documentation to complete the process.

(III)   Due to the tedious nature of their request, it would appear that the length of time to complete the application process is very long.

INVESTMENTS & OTHER WAYS

There are several other ways to raise capital. These ways could be creative in nature in order to achieve the goal of raising the funds needed for your venture. Below are examples of this type of fundraising and the mechanisms.

(17) Rotating Contribution: This type of contribution is an old school methodology of raising capital to help a member of the team. The way this works is that five or more people would choose to bind themselves in an honor system for which they would contribute money, say $1,000 each. On a monthly basis and on a specific date, let's say the 9th day of each month, everyone in this group would be required to bring their respective $1,000; no excuses and no game playing. Once the Treasurer receives the money on the 9th, the Treasurer would immediately disperse the funds to one person. Note that when you first join this team, everyone would have to agree on who would receive the money first and who will receive it next, etc. until everyone gets the money. The lump sum $5,000 would be very helpful in carrying out the venture that you need the money for.

(18) Prudent Investing - Stocks, Currency, Deals: Another way to raise capital is through capital gains and investments. These investments need to be prudent in nature with a moderate risk attached. The first example is the stock market. This is where an investor purchases the stock of a particular company based on several criteria of growth for that company. After the purchase is made, the investor awaits a particular period to sell the stock; preferably when the stock has made money. The stock market is tracked through the performance of Dow Jones industrial average. This average serves as a basis to measure corporate performance across board. In 2008, Dow Jones was at 6,600 and in 2013 Dow

Jones has peaked to 15,320. Therefore, monies invested in 2008 would have yielded high earnings by 2013.

The other type of investment is slightly more risky because of its volatility. It is the currency market. Because it holds a rather high volatile condition, many investors shy away from it. This type of investment can yield tremendous amount of money if the right strategy is supplied. A truly successful currency investor has riches in the millions. The currency market is affected by a variety of global information. For instance, between 2011 and 2012 the Euro, which is the common currency of the European nations suffered a huge set back because of certain problems experienced in Greece. When a country is facing a challenge, its currency tends to suffer severely. This is even worse when dealing with Euro because it is a currency that is maintained by several nations. So if one of the nations, experiences difficulties, then the Euro will experience difficulties as well. There is a direct and proportional relationship. Similarly, the US dollar can suffer a set back if there are political upheavals in the governmental structures. Whatever you do in the currency market, *please be careful!*

(19) Liaising - Business opportunity and Venture Capitalist: This is one of the most creative aspects of raising capital. There are several people who have the knowledge of certain things such as real estate investments and management; however, they do not have the capital to actualize their dream. Thus, because of their knowledge and because of someone else's deep pockets, they will make a good business partnership. This type of partnership can generate some very good income because of your role as a liaison. Liaisons are individuals that can detect a business opportunity and a venture capitalist. So how do you make money? You make money by bringing both together and you serve as the conduit or the linking pin of the transaction.

(20) Government Programs: The government serves as this big brother that helps the little brother in time of need. There are moments whereby everyone criticizes the government, whether justified or not. However, the government has a critical role for its people not to suffer. Insufficiency is clearly an attack against a persons' financial destiny when other avenues fail to yield the type of assistance needed, big brother could help. In 2010 and 2013 there were some great storms that passed through the Chicago land area. Many homes were flooded and as a result, several structural properties and personal items were damaged, big brother stepped in. Big brother created an agency called FEMA. FEMA is a Federal Agency Management Agency designated to assist those who were hit by disasters. As a source of capital, FEMA is sent to inspect the damages and issue cash relief. In 2010 and 2013 stated above, FEMA was helpful to me. For additional information please refer to Source of Raising Money Number 5.

(21) April Love - Tax Money: This is one of the most reliable and fun times in receiving money from the government. This is your tax refund. You are able to receive a huge refund because the government withheld money from you and because you have several deductible items. Your refund is a function of your withholdings and ability of your tax accountant to navigate tax loopholes in your favor. I call the money received during the tax period, April Love! This lump sum money received should and must not be spent on petty bills. The money received is your opportunity to start a major venture or investment. I have heard of many stories regarding the mismanagement of April Love. This must not be! This is the one time that the Federal and State governments would encourage you with cash, please be wise!

Commercial Break!

Please send your tax information to me through:

Fax: 708-401-0075
E-mail: gekhomu@aol.com

Call me @ 708-516-5259 to discuss what is
needed to complete your business tax and your
individual tax.

Chapter 8
Solution III:
Adopting a Budget

Highlights

- Principles of Budget
- Elements of Budget
- Example of Budget
- 3 Secrets of Maximizing Income

At 50, I have found that one of the major challenges I have in life is my ability and capability to stay disciplined in the things I do and in the actions I take. It seems as if every time I come across this challenge of life, I would need to pull all that is within me to muster a victory. I know that I have been created with a mindset of victory. I cannot fail. I cannot fall! Even when the winds blow, I always find a branch to hold onto so that I will not go down. I truly believe that God has set me apart for greatness. Although people may not see a physical manifestation of it, but they should look again and they will see that they are looking at one of God's creation. His name is an overcomer. I can truly and clearly say that every detail you have struggled with shall be defeated in this chapter. Budgeting is one of the most effective weapons for a person struggling with a life of insufficiency.

Ironically, like the recession the nation and the world suffered a few years back, lack of budgeting holds equal power to set someone back. That person is not you in the name of Jesus. Here we are in a Post-recession era and are poised to move forward, all of a sudden there comes another ill looking to set us back. The ill of insufficiency! We have determined that in order to appropriately move forward, we would have to apply the principles of budgeting into our daily living. As I noted in my other book (Financial Maturity After the Recession), *Budgeting is an art*. It is so because we are all compelled to perform it. Below I shall share some basic budget principles and the elements of a solid budget. I shall provide a practical budget example and where you can perform your own budget as an exercise. I have decided to lift these principles from my book in order to have a consistent teaching surrounding this topic. Please enjoy!

PRINCIPLES OF BUDGETS

(1) Management Tool to Measure Performance. It is a management tool that tends to measure performance. As a management tool, a budget looks at how budget managers perform. Each budget manager is held accountable for the resulting outcome of the budget. The resulting outcome of the budget defines the next level for that manager. The manager is either promoted for a good budget handling, or punished for mishandling the budget. My prayer is that the demon of mismanagement will be destroyed in the Name of Jesus, Amen!

> *For promotion [cometh] neither from the east, nor from the west, nor from the south* (Psalms 75:6).

The Bible notes that God has the ability to promote and demote, based on the works and your heart towards Him. You can easily assume that God rewards those who have managed His affairs diligently, and punishes those who have mismanaged it. In the story of the talents, we find that the man with one talent failed to manage properly and so his talent was taken from him and given to someone else who was able to manage the affairs of his master.

(2) Provides Guidance. As a management tool (and people tool), a budget serves as guidance. The budget is the roadmap to every financial success. A man without a roadmap normally does not do well. A roadmap is an impetus for success. It creates direction, and it provides navigation. It guides in times of difficulties. As the recession has come to an end, budgeting becomes the key player in your financial situation. It tells you when to spend and when not to. It advises you to curtail unnecessary expenses. A person with a philanthropic mind is often tempted to overspend because those in need of help are always pulling on him or her. Without this guiding tool the philanthropist might be stuck in recession whereas others are prospering. Whenever there is a doubt in your financial circumstances, please endeavor to recheck your roadmap.

(3) Budget Stresses Accountability. A society where no one is accountable is a society in chaos. A budget stresses accountability because someone needs to be held responsible for what has happened. In a family, there should be a discussion between the man and woman as to who should be responsible for the family budget. In most cases, when this decision is made and if the budget prospers, the budget owner is praised and rewarded with a family dinner or extra shopping money. On the other hand, when the budget fails, the responsible party gets blamed and the family ends up with unnecessary strife. As we all know, money is an area the enemy uses to attack the family. As such, prudence needs to be exercised in order for families to stay in harmony and remain together.

Let us say, in the Hernandez family, Mrs. Hernandez became the budget manager as agreed upon by Mr. & Mrs. Hernandez. When the budget failed, Mrs. Hernandez performed an audit of the budget. She found that Mr. Hernandez had been breaching the terms of family money spending. Mrs. Hernandez took offense to the breach and after several breaches, decided that a separation was now necessary. There are several horrible stories about budget breaches in families which end up creating relationship havoc. As a result and as a pastor, it is important for me to state that your family must be careful in the dispensation of budgeting duties and assignments.

(4) Control Mechanism. As a mechanism, the budget becomes a tool that institutes discipline in people's lives. Whenever we say there is a control mechanism, we are really talking about allowing things to be in order. As a control point, the budget master must adhere to the standards of the budget. The budget master must not sway to the left or to the right. He must remain focused, disciplined, and directed. As a controlling tool, a budget becomes a mechanism for instituting error detection in the implementation process. When large variances show up in actual dollars versus budget dollars, you'll now have a basis for good research.

(5) Realistic Projections. In the budgeting process, the budget master must learn to be candid in their projection. In a lot of cases, the budget master loses sight of the main picture. They make unrealistic projections. This unrealistic projection normally brings the budget to its knees. The fall of the budget creates financial chaos. In the period of insufficiency, you cannot operate in financial chaos. That's why it is important for you to follow the designed plans for your home and your small business.

(6) Discourage Irresponsibility. Because the budget is such an integral part of success, it is important that budget handlers are responsible in their thoughts, words and deeds. As a result of that, they cannot pass on irresponsible budgeting techniques. For your homes, whoever is handling the budget must have a record of consistent financial responsibility. This is a role that must be discharged with credibility and integrity. The character of the budget handler is important here. The Bible makes this clear in James 5:12, "*let your 'yes' be 'yes' and your 'no' be 'no'.*" This particular viewpoint in the budget process would help the family to get to the next level. Please, an irresponsible budget manager should not be allowed to manage the budget. This is important because he or she will ruin the family finances. As we deal with insufficiency as an enemy, we must ensure that the budget rules are applied strictly and enforced in order to get out of the insufficiency mess.

ELEMENTS OF A BUDGET

Due to the fact that budgeting is such an important part of a family's financial growth, it is imperative to know the elements that make up the budget.

(1) Inflow. Inflow represents the sources of funds. Your money could come from your employment, business, gifts, loans, and so on. This is the basis for the budget. For instance, if the budget master plans to collect a total of $200,000 for an annual period, that is what he should include in the budget.

(2) Outflow. This is the spending arm of the budget. The budget master gets a lot of heat about this. The budget master lists out different expenses that make up the outflow. By definition, outflow is the money that would be spent during the budget period. It is a simple concept, but one that is hard to follow.

In the example above, the budget master has several major categories to manage, including tithes, housing, family, transportation, utilities and credit cards. The danger here is that there might be items not accounted for. Normally, those expenses would create a huge variance in the budget. Therefore, the budget manager and others responsible for designing the budget should ensure a comprehensive budget is submitted.

(3) Bottom Line. This concept is easily defined as the excess of inflow over outflow; unless there is a deficit in which case outflow exceeds inflow. Everyone is supposed to support the budget in a way that the bottom line is positive.

(4) Variances. This is the difference between budget and actual. The variance is positive when the actual inflows are greater than the budgeted inflows. That means if the budget inflow is $200,000 and the actual money collected is $220,000; then there is a positive variance in the budget. In the case of expenses, if the budgeted dollars for spending or outflows exceed the actual dollars spent, that would yield a positive variance.

However, if the actual spending is greater than the budgeted spending, that would mean there is negative variance. Whenever there is a negative variance, the budget master tries hard to explain the reason behind the negative variance. As discussed in the principles of budgeting above, it is important to note that the budget column entitled "variance" is the basis for which performance is evaluated. A poor variance could get someone fired and a good variance could get them elevated.

EXAMPLE OF A BUDGET

The following is an example of a budget for the Omofoma family. It reflects that the Omofoma family received wages of about $100k from full-time employment, $50,000 from their business, and $10,000 from interest earned from deficit financing. The total income is $160,000, this is good income. The Omofoma family must not get complacent and say this is enough income; if there are additional opportunities for them to bring in more money, they must aspire accordingly.

My position in terms of aspiring for more money is that you do not allow the chase to get you derailed from the will of God. Instead of pursuing money with all your heart and soul, you should keep the words of Matthew 6:33 engraved in your palm and heart, *"But seek ye first the kingdom of God, and his righteousness; and all these things shall be added unto you."*

In this example, the Omofoma family paid 10% in tithes. In this budget, the Omofoma family ended up spending a total of $100,000 for the year and they had $60,000 left. Please see the table on the next page.

Budget for Omofoma Family
For the Year 2013

Sources of INFLOWS

Income from Wages	$100,000.00	62.50%
Income from Business	50,000.00	31.30%
Income from Interest	10,000.00	6.20%
Total Income/ INFLOWS	**$160,000.00**	**100%**

Sources of OUTFLOWS

Tithes & Offerings	$20,000.00	20%
Housing	20,000.00	20%
Food	7,500.00	7.50%
Utilities	10,000.00	10%
Transportation	7,500.00	7.50%
Credit Cards	15,000.00	15%
Other	20,000.00	20%
Total Expenses/ OUTFLOWS	**$100,000.00**	**100%**
Bottom Line	**$60,000.00**	

Please use the tabular presentation on page 105 for your budgeting template. It is important that you use the expenses that relate to you. For instance, you may not have an expense line called "Credit Cards," as such; you should not have it in your list of expenses.

Please use the following template to draw out your budget...

BONUS - 3 SECRETS OF MAXIMIZING INCOME

In March 2011, I wrote an article for the Career Resources magazine of KingsWord International Church on secrets of maximizing your income. I am led to share the 3 Secrets of Maximizing your income in this book. Enjoy!

"I introduced to the reader concepts and ideas of financial management to be explored in future editions. In that same edition, I provided an overall outlook to financial management, stating that everyone intends to do well in life because we are "wired" to be great. However, we must not squander the resources that the Lord has entrusted in our care. These resources could come in the form of full employment, inheritance, or investment; regardless of how we receive these funds we must be a good steward of it in order to be blessed more. In this edition, I shall share 3 secrets on how to maximize your income.

In our learning processes, we have been told that only corporate entities can be profitable. This is a lie from hell. You are designed and destined to be profitable and fruitful. I have found in my years of experience as a financial consultant that people become complacent in seeking to maximize their income potential. It is worthy to note that great potential resides inside of you. As such, your mess is not enough to hold you down, but it is to create a message of hope for you. As you aspire to create and maximize your income (wealth), you must remember that the Spirit of God lives within you – aka – "the hidden man" - 1 Peter 3:4.

But [let it be] the hidden man of the heart, in that which is not corruptible, [even the ornament] of a meek and quiet spirit, which is in the sight of God of great price.

Getting a full time employment is a good way to maximize your income because of the generic benefits you get. Note that it is a good start but not the optimal solution and certainly not the optimum way to utilize your time. The American corporate culture is guarded by corporate ceilings; as such you can become limited by certain corporate politics that could lead to frustrating circumstances. In addition, working a full time gig does not support your vision of owning your own business. Well, that is the goal - to own your own business and grow it into a huge entity! Yes, there are the initial struggles of turning a profit, but you must push towards a higher calling.

During the tax season, I counseled all my clients to register their own business because of the tax benefits associated with owning one. Dr. Kayode Ijisesan has been teaching on the *blessing and the pending rain.* So when the rain gets here, you must not be caught unprepared. So register a business in preparation for the blessed rain. Besides owning your business, there are other ways to maximize your income such as prudent investment.

For instance, before the inauguration of President Barack Obama, the stock market took a hard nose dive to approximately 6,600 (Dow Jones Average). Those who had foresight were able to buy certain stocks and today Dow Jones Average is at 15,122 (June 11, 2013). If you had braved that period and invested $10,000, by now you'd have made over 129% of your money. Of course the downside to this phenomenon is the risk involved.

When we are hindered by fear of failure, we would see time fly by and golden opportunities squandered. Maximizing your income takes courage plus an element of risk. You must build a relationship with the Holy Spirit within you to counsel you on when to, or not to participate in an event. Doing nothing is not an option. A vision has to drive your passion. The Prophet Habakkuk notes *"write the vision and make it plain"* (Habakkuk 2:2).

Therefore, here is a recap of the 3 secrets to maximizing your income:

(1) Full time job is good, but not optimal.

(2) Owning your own business is a great God idea. Notably in the scriptures:

> *You are the head and not the tail* (Deuteronomy 28:13).
>
> *I will bless the works of your hands* (Genesis 39:3).
>
> *Delight yourself in the Lord, and he will grant the desires of your heart* (Psalms 37:4).

(3) Risk is a necessary element you have to deal with in life; you need to understand that "*the just must life by faith*" (Romans 1:17). Your faith is bolder than any fear you might have."

Source: Ekhomu, 2011, Career Resources, KingsWord International Church.

Epilogue

Having completed the reading of this book, I am sure you have been completely blessed and ready for action. The next step is to do what you have read, that would empower you financially. Each day you practice financial sufficiency, you get better at it and you find yourself aspiring to a complete victorious living.

It all starts with one step of freedom. The practicality of this book highlights the power to overcome. According to John 1:5 when darkness saw light, it could not comprehend it; darkness disappeared, and the room was full of light. Your condition has drastically changed from insufficiency to sufficiency.

Let the reader say "Amen."

References

(1) Festus Adeyeye, *Prospering In Hard Times*. Chicago: Godkulture Publishing, 2013.

(2) Bill & Melinda Gates Foundation, the free encyclopedia. Wikipedia, June 19, 2013. [from http:// en.wikipedia.org/wiki/Gates_Foundation]

(3) Darryl Dash, *The Danger of Self-Reliance*. Toronto: Darryl's blog, 2010.

(4) Godfrey Ekhomu, *Financial Maturity After the Recession*. Chicago: Godkulture Publishing, 2011.

(5) Godfrey Ekhomu, *3 Secrets of Maximizing Your Income*. Chicago: Career Resources, KingsWord International Church, 2011.

(6) Courage Igene, *100 Reasons Why I Hate Poverty*. Chicago: Godkulture Publishing, 2013.

(7) Dora Marinova; Amzad Hossain, *Principles for Self-Reliance and Sustainability: Case Study of Bangladesh. Proceedings of the Anti-Poverty Academic Conference with International Participation, Institute for Sustainability and Technology Policy*. Perth: Murdoch University, 2006.

(8) Image on Chapter 1, Retrieved on June 23, 2013 from http://newsimg.bbc.co.uk/media/images/45054000/ jpg/_45054518_worker226.jpg

(9) Image on Chapter 2, Retrieved on June 23, 2013 from http://www.sos2day.com/images/stories/SOS_ HELP_thru_paper-_cropped.jpg

(10) Image on Chapter 3, Retrieved on June 23, 2013 from http://www.moerker.com/photography/alley.jpg

(11) Image on Chapter 4, Retrieved on June 23, 2013 from http://f.news.net/img/9/0/7/c/907c1d7534de4 cd4943a8a6d50b4cdcd-93b438ca5ac1120b2e0f6a7067 006cf7.jpg

(12) Image on Chapter 5, Retrieved on June 23, 2013 from http://www.bp.com/liveassets/bp_internet/ africa/STAGING/brand_assets/images/light_ bulb_375x200.jpg

(13) Image on Chapter 8, Retrieved on June 23, 2013 from http://blog-pfm.imf.org/.a/6a00e54ef00595883 4010536f20737970c-800wi

A New Life

Effectively *Breaking the Cycle of Insufficiency* demands that you begin a productive relationship with God and to continually *walk in abundance*, you must surrender your life to the Lordship of Jesus Christ. If you have not accepted Jesus Christ as your Lord and Savior, I encourage you to pray the following prayer aloud in order to receive your salvation.

Heavenly Father, I come to you as a sinner through Your Son, Jesus Christ who died and rose on the third day and is now seated at Your right hand. I confess all my sins and I invite Jesus into my life as my Lord and Savior. Thank You Jesus, that my sins are forgiven. Holy Spirit, I invite you to partner with me in my walk with Jesus. In Jesus name I pray. Amen!

This is the wisest decision you have ever made. Please, do not look back! Find a Bible-believing church where the unadulterated Word of God is being preached and begin to worship there regularly. Buy a Bible and study it daily.

Always ask the Holy Spirit to teach you His Word before you study. Welcome to the Kingdom of Light. May the Lord God bless and uphold you in Jesus' Mighty Name, Amen! I am waiting to hear from you. You can contact me through my address towards the end of this book, or by way of my website.

About the Author

Godfrey Ekhomu, a registered Certified Public Accountant, is the President and CEO of GOE Global Enterprise in Berkeley, Illinois. He has over 23 years of experience in accounting, finance, auditing, project management, systems and international consulting. He has worked as a consultant to various organizations (profit and nonprofit) by helping them solve complex problems and recommending sound solutions.

He leads financial empowerment & intelligence seminars for small businesses, churches and individuals. He also provides financial oversight to religious organizations, specifically in finance and information technology systems.

He serves as the lead pastor of Looking unto Jesus Global Ministry and currently worships at Kingsword International Church, Chicago. He is the author of *Financial Maturity After the Recession*, a tool that will help you become financially successful. He has an MBA from Howard University, Washington, DC, and currently completing his doctorate in Organization and Management from Capella University.

GOE Global Enterprise

GOE Global Enterprise is an Illinois-based consulting firm that provides local and global services to its clients. The services provided to individuals, for-profit organizations, as well as non-for-profit organizations include:

- Accounting, Finance & Taxation Services
- Routine Accounting Compilation & Review Services
- Consultancy and Advisory Services
- Financial Intelligence Seminars
- General Contractor – buying and selling

Contact Information

P. O. Box 2661
Northlake
IL 60164

Phone: 708-516-5259
Fax: 708-401-0075
Email: Goeglobal@aol.com
Website: www.GOEglobalenterprise.com

Looking Unto Jesus Global Ministry

Announcements

Please join us every
Thursday Night – for Bible study
Sunday Night – for Intercessory Prayers
At 8:00 PM (Central Time)
712.432.0180 access 134876

Contact Information

P. O. Box 2661
Northlake
IL 60164
Phone: 708-516-5259
Email: TBSM123@gmail.com

Looking Unto Jesus – Hebrews 12:2

Also By Godfrey O. Ekhomu

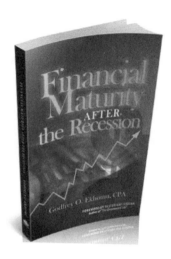

KINGDOM Economy rules!

In order to function effectively under Kingdom economy, *Financial Maturity After the Recession* charts the course of aligning you to God's will for your life and providing you essential framework to become successful in your finances.

This book comes at the nick of time, especially now that we are in a recovery phase following a devastating recession (famine). It commingles biblical principles with pragmatic financial conditions.

Scan the QR Code to purchase other Products from
Godfrey Ekhomu

Additional copies of this book and other titles from Godkulture Publishing are available at our online-retail store: **www.daforge.com** and also www.amazon.com, www.barnesandnoble.com

We are adding new titles every month!

To view our complete brochure online, visit us at: **www.Godkulturepublishing.com**

Send a request for a brochure to:

GODKULTURE
PUBLISHING

1830 South Allport Street
Chicago
IL 60608
USA

Phone: 773-696-0008

"Covering the Earth with the Knowledge of God's Glory"

Are you an author?

Do you have a God-inspired message?

CONTACT US

We'll be glad to review your manuscript for the likelihood of publication:

publishing@Godkulture.org